1.9

Lots of
Grandparents

Lots of Grandparents

by Shelley Rotner and Sheila Kelly, Ed.D.

Photographs by Shelley Rotner

THE MILLBROOK PRESS M BROOKFIELD, CONNECTICUT

Grandmothers, Grandfathers;
Nanas, Papas;
Memes, Pepes;
Bathis, Jajus;

Abuelos, Abuelas;
Gukas, Shoshos;
Poppys, Babas.

There are lots of grandparents and even
great-grandparents.

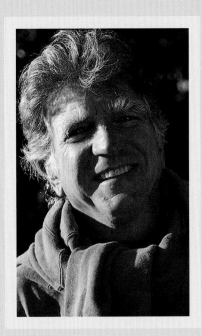

Sometimes they come to visit,

or you visit them.

Sometimes grandparents
take care of you.

They tell you stories,
share their treasures . . .

and give you presents and treats.

They like to play with you . . .

. . . and are proud of what
you can do.

Some grandparents look old and have wrinkles; some don't.

Some move very slowly; some don't.

Some don't see very well.
Some don't hear very well.

Some can't walk very well.
And some have trouble breathing.

Sometimes they live where there are people to take care of them.

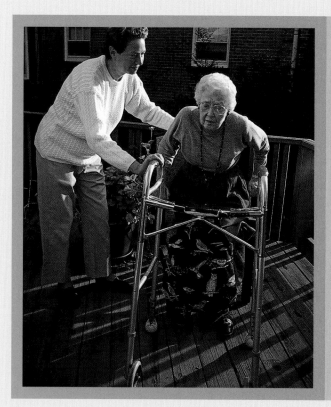

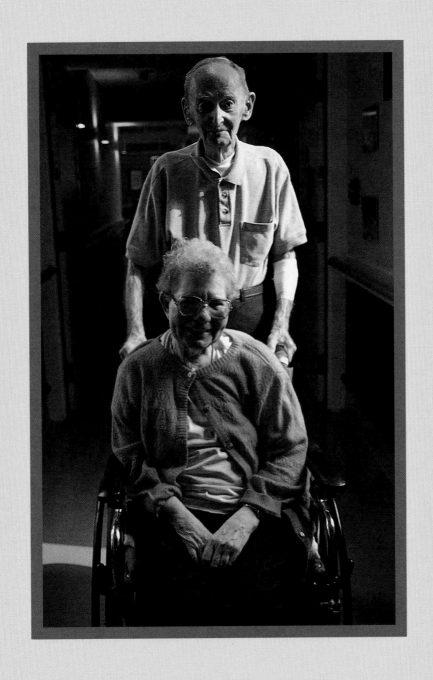

They have friends there and help
each other when they can.

Some grandparents go to work.

Some work at home.

They like to be busy.

And they like to have fun!

Best of all, grandparents love their grandchildren.

It's good there are lots of grandparents!

*In loving memory of
my grandmother.* —SR

*For Ella Kelly, our great Gan,
and all her friends at Upper Canada Lodge in
Niagra-on-the-Lake.* —SK

We're grateful to the grandparents and their grandchildren who helped create this book.

Lots of Grandparents
Copyright © 2001 by Shelley Rotner and Sheila Kelly Photographs copyright © 2001 by Shelley Rotner
All rights reserved

Published by The Millbrook Press, Inc.
2 Old New Milford Road, Brookfield, Connecticut 06804
www.millbrookpress.com

Printed in the United States of America
5 4 3 2 1

Library of Congress Cataloging-in-Publication Data

Rotner, Shelley
Lots of grandparents/Shelley Rotner and Sheila Kelly; photographs
by Shelley Rotner.
p. cm.
ISBN 0-7613-2313-9 (lib. bdg.)
1. Grandparents—Juvenile literature. 2. Grandparent and
child—Juvenile literature. [1. Grandparents.] I. Kelly, Sheila M. II.
Title.

HQ759.9 .R68 2001
306.874′ 5—dc21
00-066827